CHRIST'S VOICE
A NEW LECTIONARY FOR THE CHURCH

BISHOP HUGH GILBERT, OSB

All booklets are published
thanks to the generosity of the supporters
of the Catholic Truth Society

Contents

First published 2024
by The Incorporated Catholic Truth Society
42-46 Harleyford Road London SE11 5AY
Tel: 020 7640 0042. *www.ctsbooks.org*

ISBN 978-1-78469-806-5

All biblical quotations are taken from the ESV-CE.

Introduction: Unrolling the Scroll

> And he came to Nazareth, where he had been brought up. And as was his custom, he went to the synagogue on the sabbath, and he stood up to read. He unrolled the scroll and found the place where it was written,
>
> "The Spirit of the Lord is upon me,
> because he has anointed me
> to proclaim good news to the poor." (*Luke* 4:16-18)

For St Luke, this is a turning point in the Gospel. Jesus, having been baptised by John and overcome the testing of Satan, begins his public ministry by reading a programmatic text from the prophet Isaiah at the Sabbath synagogue service in Nazareth. From this action flows the whole public ministry of Jesus. There is something particularly arresting in the mention of Jesus physically "unrolling the scroll". The Word made flesh took a scroll into his hands and read out the words written on it. This scroll (of papyrus or parchment presumably) has long since crumbled into dust, but the Lord's proclamation has not. It continues. It remains alive. "Today", he added, "this Scripture has been fulfilled in your hearing" (*Luke* 4:21). What was really being "unrolled" here was the purpose of God: the coming of his Kingdom, the advent of the Messiah.

This dramatic passage throws our minds forward to another biblical opening of a scroll – that recounted in the Book of Revelation. Now we are no longer in a synagogue on earth, but in the throne-room of heaven. John the Seer, more commonly known as John the Evangelist, sees a scroll in the right hand of the one seated on the throne, that is, God the Father. It is a scroll sealed with seven seals. It contains the mystery of God's plan for human history and its consummation. To John's dismay, there seems no one capable of opening it – until he sees "a lamb standing as if he had been slain, with seven horns and seven eyes" (*Rev* 5:6). This is the crucified and risen Christ, replete with power and knowledge. He can open the mysterious scroll, breaking its seals one by one. Just as the whole ministry of Jesus in the Gospel of Luke flows from his act of unrolling the scroll in the synagogue of Nazareth, so in a sense the whole revelation of the "last things" that fill the Apocalypse flows from the Lamb's breaking the seals of the scroll he has received from God's right hand.

On the first Sunday of Advent 2024, throughout England, Wales and Scotland, a new Lectionary comes into force. Countless readers at ambos in churches throughout the country will open newly published books and proclaim the word of the Lord. This will be a continuation and an echo of what the Lord did in Nazareth and does in heaven. It is the same event of the unfolding of the mystery, the plan, of God. It is Christ the Lector, Christ the Word in action.

"He [Christ] is always present in his word since it is he himself who speaks when the holy scriptures are read in the Church," said the Second Vatican Council (*Sacrosanctum Concilium* 7[1]). And again, "... [I]n the liturgy God speaks to his people and Christ still proclaims the Gospel" (*SC* 33).

A new Lectionary is a fresh chance to hear Christ speaking to us with the ears of faith; to take a fresh look at the Liturgy of the Word; to sense the "living and active" quality of God's word (*Heb* 4:12); to let it bring us together with others; and to incorporate it more into our lives.

It can help us share the aspiration of St Ignatius of Antioch not to be a mere sound, but "a word of God" (*Letter to the Romans*, 2).

---

[1] *Sacrosanctum Concilium* hereafter abbreviated SC.

This booklet seeks to address some of the questions that naturally arise with the advent of a new liturgical book, and such a major one:

- Why a new Lectionary?
- What is a Lectionary?
- What is the Liturgy of the Word?
- Why this version of Scripture? And why this new version of the Psalms?
- What is done in other parts of the Catholic world?
- What will it ask of us and what will it bring us?

What is the Liturgy of the Word?

A Lectionary is only an instrument. It is an instrument at the service of the Liturgy of the Word. A new Lectionary provides a golden opportunity for a fresh appreciation of what is happening in the Liturgy of the Word.

Pope Francis has expressed the power and beauty of the Liturgy thus:

> If the resurrection were for us a concept, an idea, a thought; if the Risen One were for us the recollection of the recollection of others, however authoritative, as, for example, of the Apostles; if there were not given also to us the possibility of a true encounter with Him, that would be to declare the newness of the Word made flesh to have been all used up. Instead, the Incarnation, in addition to being the only always new event that history knows, is also the very method that the Holy Trinity has chosen to open to us the way of communion. Christian faith is either an encounter with Him alive, or it does not exist.

> The Liturgy guarantees for us the possibility of such an encounter (*Desiderio Desideravi* 10-11[5]).

The Liturgy is the "today" of salvation.

> The salvific power of the sacrifice of Jesus, his every word, his every gesture, glance, and feeling reaches us through the celebration of the sacraments…It is the concrete way, by means of his incarnation, that he loves us. It is the way in which he satisfies his own thirst for us that he had declared from the cross. (*John* 19:28) (*DD* 11).

What is true of Christ's presence and action in the Liturgy as a whole is also true, in its specific way, when the word of God is being proclaimed. When the Lord read from the scroll of Isaiah in the synagogue in Nazareth, he said "Today this Scripture is being fulfilled in your hearing." The same can be said when Scripture is proclaimed in the liturgical assembly. Scripture is being fulfilled; it is passing from text to reality; it is becoming incarnate in those who listen to and obey it, who make themselves rich and receptive soil for it.

> God, who spoke in the past, continues to converse with the spouse of his beloved Son. And the Holy Spirit, through whom the living voice of the Gospel rings out in the Church – and through it in the world – leads believers to the full truth and makes the word

[5] *Desiderio Desideravi* hereafter abbreviated DD.

of Christ dwell in them in all its richness (cf. *Col* 3:16) (*DV* 8).

This sense of Christ still proclaiming the word reaches its climax with the reading of the Gospel. Many surrounding rites highlight this, e.g. the reservation of the proclamation to the ordained, the posture of standing, the acclamation which precedes the reading and "by which the gathering of the faithful welcomes and greets the Lord who is about to speak to them" (*General Instruction of the Roman Missal, for England and Wales and Scotland*, n. 62). "The Gospel is the mouth of Christ", said St Augustine. "He is seated at the right hand of the Father, yet continues to speak on earth" (*Sermon* 85:1). In the Liturgy of St John Chrysostom, used in the Byzantine rite, the cry "Wisdom! Stand upright. Let us listen to the Holy Gospel. Peace to all" precedes the reading.

The Liturgy of the Word is Christ himself coming among us, and this reaches its climax when his Gospel is proclaimed. A strong sense of these things led Pope Benedict XVI, in his Apostolic Exhortation *Verbum Domini*, to speak *of the sacramentality of the word.*

The sacramentality of the word can thus be understood by analogy with the real presence of Christ under the appearances of the consecrated bread and wine. By approaching the altar and partaking in the Eucharistic banquet we truly share in the body and blood of Christ. The proclamation of God's word at the celebration entails an acknowledgment that Christ himself is present, that he speaks to us, and that he wishes to be heard. St Jerome speaks of the way we ought to approach both the Eucharist and the word of God: "We are reading the sacred Scriptures. For me, the Gospel is the Body of Christ; for me, the holy Scriptures are his teaching. And when he says: *whoever does not eat my flesh and drink my blood* (*John* 6:53), even though these words can also be understood of the [Eucharistic] Mystery, Christ's body and blood are really the word of Scripture, God's teaching. When we approach the [Eucharistic] Mystery, if a crumb falls to the ground we are troubled. Yet when we are listening to the word of God, and God's Word and Christ's flesh and blood are being poured into our ears yet we pay no heed, what great peril should we not feel?" (St Jerome, *On Psalm 147*). Christ, truly present under the species of bread and wine, is analogously present in the word proclaimed in the liturgy (*VD* 56).

Metaphors and Meanings

If the Liturgy is the "today" of salvation, it always includes what has gone before it. In the Liturgy of the Word, then, the great occasions of the word's proclamation remain alive. We can think of how Moses read the Law at the foot of the mountain and sealed the covenant with the sprinkling of blood (*Ex* 24). Or how the Law was read again after the people's return from the Babylonian exile

(*Neh* 8). In Deuteronomy 31, Moses prescribed a public reading of the Law in the hearing of all Israel every seven years at the Feast of Tabernacles. Sabbath after Sabbath, the Jewish people could, and can, hear God's word read in the synagogue liturgy. In the Christian Liturgy of the Word, the prophets and the apostles preach again and, above all, the Lord re-enacts for us that ministry of the word which began after his Baptism and ended in the Upper Room "on the night he was betrayed". During the Liturgy of the Word, we are seated on the shore of the Lake or in the synagogue of Capernaum, in the house of Martha, Mary and Lazarus or in the Temple precincts. The Liturgy of the Word is the ongoing proclamation of the Kingdom of God. May we hear it and be changed!

The Liturgy of the Word, therefore, is the mother of unity. Through the acts of reading and listening, the physical gathering of the people becomes a spiritual gathering. A deeper unity is brought about. In many monasteries books are read aloud during mealtime. The texts heard together create a common culture in the community; they unify. How much more the Spirit-filled proclaiming of the word Sunday after Sunday! As Pope Francis has said:

> The Bible is the book of the Lord's people, who, in listening to it, move from dispersion and division towards unity. The word of God unites believers and makes them one people (*Aperuit Illis* 4).

In the Liturgy of the Word, the Church prepares for us "the Table of the Word" – the first table at which the Church is brought together and nourished by the many words that come from the mouth of God. St Charles de Foucauld believed that in Scripture God has a word for each person, the particular food they need in their journey through the wilderness.

Again, this Liturgy is a "school of listening", a moment when what St Benedict calls "the ear of the heart" is opened by the Holy Spirit. The process of synodality has raised awareness of this need for listening, and first of all to the Lord. "O that today you would listen to his voice! Harden not your hearts" (*Ps* 95:7-8). It is therefore the first "school of Christian prayer". Here God speaks to us through his word and we listen and respond. This is the original "conversation in the Spirit". The structure is that of a dialogue. The reading is answered by an acclamation or the verse of a Psalm; the advent of the Gospel reading is hailed and signs of reverence surround it. The readings and the homily are met with the Profession of Faith and the common Prayer of the Faithful. The initiative is divine and the response is ours, but in that response the Holy Spirit too is at work.

In the Liturgy of the Word, the Sower still goes out to sow his seed. "The seed is the word of God" (*Luke* 8:11). Some falls on the path, some on rock, some among thorns, some on good soil. "As for that in the good soil, they are those who, hearing the word, hold it fast in an honest and good heart, and bear fruit with patience" (*Luke* 8:15).

The Liturgy of the Word, to suggest another metaphor, is the marital "conversation" of Christ the Bridegroom and his Bride the Church – a conversation which prepares for the further intimacy proper to the Eucharist.

The lives of the Saints illustrate the power of the liturgical word. It was when St Anthony the Great heard the words of the Gospel of St Matthew in church that he embarked on the monastic life and created a new expression of Christianity in the world. The Liturgy of the Word is not a mere replay of the past – the reading out of ancient texts – it regenerates and transforms.

In the Liturgy of the Eucharist, we are close to the Mother of Jesus as she stood by the cross of her son. In the Liturgy of the Word, we can share her open ear and pondering heart.

Why this Version of the Bible? What is the English Standard Version?

The English Standard Version (ESV) was born in the 1990s, amid a general flurry of new translations. It was the collaborative fruit of a team of some one hundred plus biblical scholars, overseen by a Translation Oversight Committee of twelve members. These scholars were largely American and of a range of backgrounds within the Evangelical world. It was published by the American Christian publisher Crossway in 2001, with subsequent editions appearing in 2007, 2011 and 2016.

Bible translations are often "family affairs" rather than isolated items. The ESV belongs to the oldest and most venerable of these in the English-speaking world, that stemming from the King James Bible or Authorised Version of 1611. Since the late nineteenth century, this tradition has produced several offspring, of which the best-known and most widely used in the twentieth century was the Revised Standard Version (RSV), itself last revised in 1971. Catholic editions of the RSV have been used in several Lectionaries of the English-speaking world since the 1960s, including Britain and Ireland (alongside the Jerusalem Bible).

The ESV represents a further shoot from this stock. It is a revision of the RSV, enough of such to merit a new name, making some 60,000 changes to its predecessor, i.e. affecting about 8% of its mother text.

The intention of the ESV was to produce a Bible both accurate and beautiful. It takes care to incorporate the latest scholarship regarding the original Hebrew, Greek and Aramaic texts. So far as there is a divide between what translators call "formally equivalent" versions, which privilege transparency to the original texts, and "dynamically equivalent" ones, which privilege comprehensibility to those using the text, the ESV falls resolutely on the side of the former. At the same time, it recognises the balance that must always be struck between "taking the people to the Bible" and "taking the Bible to the people", between being "source-orientated" and "target-orientated". Most of its changes to the RSV are in fact modernisations (for example, eliminating "thou's" and "thee's", replacing "yonder" with "over there", and such-like).

Fidelity to the original languages is the principle the ESV uses to pick its way through the controversial terrain of "inclusive language". The latter, therefore, is not made a criterion in itself, which will disappoint some, but this principled approach interestingly yields a text which is markedly more sensitive to the gender-specific than the RSV (and, in a Catholic context, the Jerusalem Bible). "The extent to which inclusive language has been incorporated into the ESV will surprise many people", wrote the commentator Rodney Decker three years after its first publication. The basic intentions of the ESV translation are outlined more fully in its preface.

No translation is perfect and none will engage all readers. "Each has his own gift from God, one of one kind, one of another" (*1 Cor* 7:7). What St Paul said of members of the Christian community could be said of the more than 350 translations of the Bible that the Anglosphere has produced over the centuries: "each has his own gift". What, then, is the "gift" of the ESV? It can legitimately claim to be a Bible based on quality textual scholarship, an indispensable requirement. It is also grounded on a robust sense of Scripture's divine worth, a point further developed below. While respecting the diversity of the various books that comprise the Bible, it also has a strong grasp of the ultimate unity of Scripture and of Christ as the source of that unity. As a source-orientated translation, it shows respect for and aims at transparency to the original languages. It can be refreshingly precise. It therefore "harvests" more of the complex meanings and imagery of the Bible and allows the culture of the biblical world to stay with us. While adjusting to contemporary usage, it attempts to keep both the classical English tradition of Bible translation and theological terminology alive. Time will assess its success. It is not the work of an individual, however gifted, but of many, a collaborative venture as the complexity of modern scholarship demands. It comes from a particular Evangelical stable, certainly, but its publishers have shown a cautious openness to its adoption by other traditions. This resonates with the encouragement found in Catholic circles, from *Dei Verbum* onwards, of translations which are ecumenically acceptable.

Vatican II's Decree on Ecumenism could not have put the last point more forcibly: "the sacred Word is a precious instrument in the mighty hand of God for attaining to that unity which the Saviour holds out to all" (*Unitatis Redintegratio*, 21).

Some specifics

It may be useful to flesh out these generalities with some specifics. There is a case, surely, for a Bible that in Genesis 1:2 has "the *Spirit* of God" hovering over the face of the waters, that allows Isaiah 7:14 to speak of *the virgin* conceiving, that has Jesus echo the divine name by calling out on the waters *It is I* (*Mark* 6:50), rather than "It's me!", and in Romans 9:5 allows St Paul to proclaim unequivocally *the Christ, who is God over all.*

The effort to retain Hebrew idioms is also welcome. If Adam "*knew* his wife Eve" (*Gen* 4:1) rather than "had intercourse" with her, and if Joseph "*knew* [Mary] not" (*Matt* 1:25) rather than "had not had intercourse with her", not only is the delicacy of the Hebrew retained but the expression '*to know the Lord*' used in other contexts can be recognised for the nuptial expression it is (e.g. *Hos* 2:22 and *Jer* 31:33-34).

One scholar has pointed out how well the ESV picks up the specificity of Numbers 12:8 where the Lord says he speaks to Moses, not merely "face to face" as in Exodus 33:11, but *mouth to mouth*. (This is almost invariably missed). Thus connections are formed with Deuteronomy 8:3: "man lives by every word that comes from the *mouth* of the Lord", with the quotation of Psalm 78:2 in Matthew 13:35: "I will open my *mouth* in parables" and not least with Matthew 5:3 where the Incarnate Word, seated on the mountain, "opened his *mouth* and taught them, saying..." (missed in the RNJB's bland "began to speak"). As Fr Joseph O'Hanlon beautifully expresses it: "God speaking the words of healing, of saving, of helping 'mouth to mouth', is the God who embraces with a kiss of concern and heals with a kiss of love the pain of humanity. Jesus opens his mouth and speaks words that heal, words that gospel the world to safe harbour."

In the Johannine Discourse on the Bread of Life there is an effort to register the significant change in verbs

> The books of the Old and New Testament, whole and entire, with all their parts...[are] written under the inspiration of the Holy Spirit, have God as their author, and have been handed on as such to the Church herself...Since then, all that the inspired authors, or sacred writers, affirm should be regarded as affirmed by the Holy Spirit, we must acknowledge that the books of Scripture firmly, faithfully and without error, teach that truth which God, for the sake of our salvation, wished to see confided to the sacred Scriptures.

Catholics and Protestants may verbalise their understanding of the divine authorship, inspiration and truthfulness of Scripture in different ways and disagree about the role of Tradition, but they come together in this core conviction. And such a conviction provides vital underpinning for a version of the Bible that will speak with power in the liturgical assembly. The sense of the sacredness of Scripture pervades the ESV as a whole and will discreetly permeate its proclamation.

The ESV/ESV-CE shares another Catholic conviction too, that of the unity of Scripture. As St Augustine concisely expressed it, the New Testament lies hidden in the Old and the Old is fully revealed in the New. There is a reciprocal "involvement" of the two Testaments, of which Christ is its author, supremely through his Paschal mystery. In the last chapter of the St Luke's Gospel, we see the Lord giving the "fuller" or "spiritual sense" of Scripture to the Church in the persons of the first disciples (*Luke* 24:27, 45-48). This principle, or rather gift, underlies the relating of readings from the Old Testament to the New which structures the Lectionary. It should also inform the preaching of homilies, a point beautifully developed in nn. 16-25 of the *Homiletic Directory* of 2014. The ESV/ESV-CE lends itself to this. Thus the ESV, by the way it renders the blessing of the Gentiles that will flow from Abraham (understanding the references of Genesis as an action of God), harmonises perfectly with the "take" on these texts in the New Testament preaching of Ss. Peter and Paul (*Acts* 3:25; *Gal* 3:8). Neither, as already mentioned, is the ESV reluctant to render the relevant Hebrew in Isaiah 7:14 as "a virgin shall conceive" in order to strengthen the link to Matthew 1:23, and so bind Old Testament prophecy and New Testament fulfilment (as does the RNJB). It is good to note too that the new Psalter translates Psalm 16:10b as "nor let your holy one see corruption", which will connect seamlessly with the ESV translation of the same verse in Acts 2:27, 31 and 13:35. It is thus signalled that the Psalm's "holy one" rescued from the corruption of the grave was a pointer to the resurrected Lord. These are only three instances among others, but they demonstrate how comfortably the ESV/ESV-CE (and the Abbey Psalter) fit with a liturgical and theological sensibility that is classically Catholic.

The great work of translating into the vernacular languages that the Council required has proved to be a learning process for the Church. It has not been without mistakes and controversies. But through it one great truth has become clear, namely that liturgy has its own semantic field and rhetorical registers and its own style. Of course, it must be accessible to those taking part, and it is in finding the balance between fidelity to the original text and to the language and understanding of those who will make it their own that the art of translation lies, as Pope Francis implied in his 2017 *Letter to Cardinal Sarah*. But clearly, liturgical language has its own history and culture, dignity and resonance, and these require respect. As with other liturgical texts, so with Scriptural readings within the liturgy. While the ESV/ESV-CE naturally aims at comprehensibility and avoids unnecessary archaisms, it is keen to show a deep reverence for the specific "world" of biblical language, and indeed for how that has been carried over in the English tradition. In this respect too, it should be liturgy-friendly.

A small but telling instance of this is the rendering of John 1:29: "Behold, the Lamb of God, who takes away the sin of the world" (rather than, "Look, there is..." as in the RNJB), and the echo of it we hear before Holy Communion: "Behold the Lamb of God, behold him who takes away the sins of the world".

The Church's assimilative power

A final point here might evoke St John Henry Newman's sense of the "assimilative power" of dogmatic truth and sacramental grace or, more simply, of the Church. This is Christianity's capacity to take on things that might appear extra-mural, other than or even alien to its own traditions, and in taking them on make them its own. A re-framing occurs which, while discarding what is incompatible, assimilates the positivities. The "reception" of Evagrius and Origen into the classical spiritual tradition of the Church would be an example from the early centuries. Many others could be cited. Something analogous surely recurs in the domain that concerns us here. One could instance Bishop Richard Challoner's use of the Authorised Version to enhance the Catholic Douay version, or the acceptance of so much Protestant or Anglican biblical scholarship by the scholars who produced the *Bible de Jérusalem*, or the Catholic adoption from the 1960s onwards of the Revised Standard Version. The same dynamic is at work in the adoption of the ESV – not only in the fact of a Catholic edition, but more profoundly in its being handed over to the divine energies proper to the sacramental liturgy of the Church. This offers a welcome that transforms and enables a mutual enrichment of charisms. This is all in accord with both the letter and spirit of the Second Vatican Council. It is something Catholic.

And why this new version of the Psalms?

"How good to sing Psalms to our God; how pleasant to chant fitting praise!" (*Ps* 147:1).

The Psalms play a key role in Christian worship in general and in the Lectionary also. They are used daily in every celebration of the Liturgy of the Word at Mass, something that cannot be said of any other biblical book. They are also the only Old Testament texts used in Eastertide, which otherwise restricts itself to those of the New Testament. The entrance and communion antiphons in the Roman Missal regularly draw on the Psalms. Crucially too, the Psalms are the only part of Scripture that the people as a whole will voice aloud, during the Responsorial Psalm.

The previous Lectionary, based on the Jerusalem Bible, did not use the Jerusalem Bible Psalms, but what were known as the Grail Psalms. Similarly, the new Lectionary will not draw its Psalmody from the ESV but make use of the Revised Grail Psalter (RGP), more commonly known as the Abbey Psalter.

The Grail Psalms of 1963 have served us well. Back in the day, they introduced countless Catholics to the original "prayer-book of the Church". They were hailed by C S Lewis and others. Their sprung rhythm and many felicitous turns of phrase lent themselves to singing and memorising. Much of their content remains in the RGP that will replace them. This new Psalter is the work, since

1998, of the Benedictine monks of Conception Abbey, Missouri, under the direction of Abbot Gregory Polan. It also includes revised versions of the Old and New Testament Canticles used in the Liturgy of the Hours. Hence its other title of Abbey Psalms and Canticles. It has been much worked on since its initial form and was finally approved for the United States of America in 2018. It is expected that it will feature in revised versions of the Liturgy of the Hours, as well as in many English-language versions of the Lectionary.

The need for a revision of the original Grail Psalter was voiced by several sources. The desire to give that translation strict rhythmic patterns, similar to those of the Hebrew, required abbreviations and paraphrases in many verses. This entailed some loss of the biblical imagery. An example occurs in Psalm 63 (62):2, which currently reads: "O God, you are my God, for you I long; for you my soul is thirsting". This has its own beauty and is familiar as the opening of the first Psalm of Sunday Morning Prayer in the Divine Office. However, it omits the reference in the original Hebrew to "dawn". The RGP version therefore reads, "O God, you are my God; at dawn I seek you; for you my soul is thirsting." It is good to retrieve "dawn", as it explains why this Psalm is prayed at the Morning Office and strengthens the reference to the Resurrection of the Lord. It was as dawn approached that the women would discover the empty tomb. The

Psalmist, rising early, was unconsciously anticipating the wonder to come.

This Psalter may at times have less of the poetic and rhythmic charm of the version it is replacing, but it is sustained by an intention of eliciting the fuller richness of the text and by an understanding of Hebrew rhetoric and how best to incorporate Hebrew style into English. Our musicians are already rising to the challenge, for example, Dr Matthew Ward's new setting of the Psalmody, *Psalms for All Seasons.*

The numbering of the Psalms can be done in one of two ways: following the Hebrew text (as the Authorised Version does) or following the Greek Septuagint's text. The Lectionary will follow the way the Hebrew text numbers the Psalms while noting in brackets the numbering of the Septuagint and the Vulgate.

What Happens Elsewhere?

It is sometimes good to look over the garden fence.

Revisions of the Lectionary have occurred in several parts of the world in recent years. For example, new versions of the French (2014) and Spanish (2017) Lectionaries.

The map of the Anglophone world is as follows:

The USA and the Philippines use the Revised New American Bible (RNAB), and the USA has adopted the RGP for its Psalms.

India, Malaysia, Singapore and Brunei use the ESV-CE and the RGP.

In cooperation with one another, Ireland, Australia and New Zealand are moving away from the Jerusalem Bible (JB) and probably towards the Revised New Jerusalem Bible (RNJB).

In the ecclesiastical territories of South Africa, Swaziland, Botswana, Ghana, Nigeria, Uganda, Kenya, Zimbabwe, Lesotho and some other areas in sub-Saharan English-speaking Africa, the second Catholic Edition of the Revised Standard Version (RSV-2CE) and the RGP are used. It is the same in the Antilles, i.e. the Caribbean and adjacent territories.

Canada uses the New Revised Standard Version (NRSV).

The wide variety is noteworthy here, as is also the common usage of the RSV, NRSV and ESV "family". The choice of the ESV-CE in our own part of the world is hardly unique.

What Will the New Lectionary Ask of Us and What Will It Bring Us?

It will of course be a change and change can be irritating, especially when it turns on small things like the order of words in a familiar phrase or the response to a Psalm. It will require patience. It will take time to get used to. An attitude of welcome will help us through these initial difficulties.

A version of Scripture that highlights closeness to the original text is more demanding on the listener than those which prioritise being more accessible. It is "more challenging to read and to understand since it does not try to explain everything. It requires more of the reader, the preacher, and the interpreter, but it also promises more by being as transparent as possible to the original meaning".[6] It is important to be conscious of this "more".

---

[6] Mark Giszczak, *Bible Translation and the Making of the ESV Catholic Edition*, Augustine Institute, Greenwood Village, CO, 2022, p. 112.

Readers

In a Motu Proprio of 15 January 2021, *Spiritus Domini*, Pope Francis modified Canon Law in order to allow women, as well as men, to be instituted as Lectors. We have already long experienced the reading of Scripture at the Liturgy by both men and women. This of course will continue. Pope Francis's innovation is to allow also, for those who are called to it and meet the criteria which Bishops' Conferences will spell out, the possibility of being *instituted as readers* (or acolytes). This is based, not on ordained ministry, but on the baptismal priesthood common to all the faithful.

The essential point is to value the act of reading in the Liturgy of the Word. We have all had experience of readings well read and of those not so, and we know the difference it makes. Aside from the necessary personal qualities required – not least a certain self-effacement – clear enunciation, pronunciation and understanding of the structure and meaning of the text are important; adequate preparation is also important. The need for more preparation arises from the following characteristics of the new scriptural version: its faithfulness to the structure and wording of the original text along with its sensitivity to the tradition of scriptural translation. A case in point is certain passages of the Letters of St Paul (himself capable of being "hard to understand" according to *2 Peter* 3:16!): some passages are "rough" and require thought on the part of the reader in order to convey the correct interpretation to the listeners.

More important still is a sense of the liturgical context in which the reading occurs. Any reading is at the service of a dialogue between God and man, Christ and his Church. It is not a personal performance, not even just the communication of a message; it is an act of divine worship into which both reader and listener are drawn by the Holy Spirit.

Deacons

It is the task of the deacon, when present, to proclaim the Gospel during the Liturgy of the Word. He too will need to prepare so that Christ's voice may resound through him.

The homilist

Turning to the homilist, mention has already been made of the usefulness, in the context of the new Lectionary, of the 2014 *Homiletic Directory* of the then Congregation for Divine Worship and the Discipline of the Sacraments. The homily is a favourite theme of Pope Francis, and he treats it extensively and vigorously in nn. 135-159 of the Apostolic Exhortation *Evangelii Gaudium*. It is always an examination of conscience for a preacher to re-read this.

As noted above, a translation that prioritises transparency to the original text and is therefore source-oriented also asks "more" of the homilist, be he deacon, priest or bishop. The Bible comes from another culture than ours, and it may already be true that we are less familiar with Scripture than our recent forbears. It is "other" at a higher level too:

> For my thoughts are not your thoughts, neither are your ways my ways, declares the Lord. For as the heavens are higher than the earth, so are my ways higher than your ways, and my thoughts than your thoughts (*Isa* 55:8-9).

There is a transcendence to Scripture. It is the task of the homilist to throw a bridge (or a Jacob's ladder?) over any gap there may be, and on that bridge to create two-way traffic, both bringing the people to Scripture and Scripture to the people. The value of a more literal approach, to say it one last time, is that it allows more of the complexity and richness of Scripture to reach us. If we find ourselves occasionally baffled or affronted by the word of God, even in its human language, we may not be so far from the kingdom of God. The new Lectionary is a chance to enter our inheritance, the strange, many-splendoured thing which is the biblical word of God.

Above all, though, the homily is a continuation of that dialogue which is the essence of the Liturgy of the Word and culminates in the Eucharist. Pope Francis affirms this in *Evangelii Gaudium*:

> It is worth remembering that "the liturgical proclamation of the word of God, especially in the eucharistic assembly, is not so much a time for

meditation and catechesis as a dialogue between God and his people, a dialogue in which the great deeds of salvation are proclaimed and the demands of the covenant are continually restated" [John Paul II]. The homily has special importance due to its eucharistic context: it surpasses all forms of catechesis as the supreme moment in the dialogue between God and his people which lead up to sacramental communion. The homily takes up once more the dialogue which the Lord has already established with his people. The preacher must know the heart of his community, in order to realise where its desire for God is alive and ardent, as well as where that dialogue, once loving, has been thwarted and is now barren (*Evangelii Gaudium* 137).

And to what can it bring us all?

In a word, Christ. In a phrase, "the surpassing worth of knowing Christ Jesus" (*Phil* 3:8).

Conclusion: Extinguishing the Lamps

From hearing to sight

In his thirty-fifth Homily on the Gospel of St John, St Augustine quotes 2 Peter on "the prophetic word", the inspired scriptures. This word, says St Peter, is something "to which you will do well to pay attention as to a lamp shining in a dark place, until the day dawns and the morning star rises in your hearts" (*2 Pet* 1:19). For St Augustine, this dawning day is the final coming of Christ, and the hope of it lifts his heart and his prose:

> Then, when that day has come, there will be no need of lamps. Then we shall have no reading from the prophets. The epistles of Paul will stay unopened. We shall not require the witness of John. We shall not even need the Gospel. So all the scriptures will be put aside, the scriptures which in the darkness of this age shine like lamps for us so that we are not left in the shadows (*Homily* 35).

The scrolls will be rolled up. What shall we see then, he asks? What will we see when we can see what those who wrote the Scriptures are seeing now? Let us love, he says. Let us run together in faith towards this fullness of seeing. What shall we see then?

> You will come to the fountain from which flows the water with which you have been sprinkled. You will see that light in all its clarity from which fitful and broken gleams shone into your hearts while it was in darkness here below. You are being made pure that you may see (*Homily* 35).

So as we wait for the day we cherish the lamplight. We "attend" to the prophetic word of Scripture. It suffices for our common journey as the pilgrim people of God. "We do not blindly seek God, or wait for him to speak to us first." He has already spoken. "Let us receive the sublime treasure of the revealed word" (Pope Francis, *Evangelii Gaudium* 175).

This, of course, is what our Lady did. With her prayers, may our new Lectionary help us to do the same.